MW01244858

prayers and reflection
A 90 DAY JOURNAL

Copyright © 2019
All rights reserved. This book or any portion thereof
may not be reproduced or used in any manner whatsoever
without express written permission except for
the use of brief quotations in a book review.

Scriptures are taken from the
KING JAMES VERSION, public domain
and WORLD ENGLISH BIBLE, public domain.

Printed in the United States of America
First Printing, 2019

USE THIS JOURNAL TO STRENGTHEN
your faith,
GIVE THANKS FOR
your blessings,
AND WORK TOWARD
your daily goals.

Here are some real world examples
of how you might use the daily spread:

Lord,

hear my prayers...

* for our financial situation to be less stressful
* Grammy's health
* to strengthen our marriage
* MRI test results
* lessen my anxiety

guide me to...

* be more empathetic towards others
* be patient with our children – they are trying.

keep me grateful for...

* the home we live in
* today's weather – it was beautiful!!
* my parents, who are always helping us with the kids

help me hear your answers...

!!!!!!! John's cancer is in remission !!!!!!!

Monday, Feb 25, 2019
today's date

goals & notes for today

8:00 AM – Doctors Appointment
11:30 AM – Lunch w/ Stacy @ Cafe on the Corner
3:30 PM – Girls have gymnastics practice

Don't Forget to fill out permission slip
for field trip – DUE ON THURSDAY!!

Groceries:
- ☑ milk
- ☑ butter
- ☐ applesauce pouches
- ☐ protein powder
- ☐ cereal
- ☐ peanut butter
- ☐ jelly

ASK, AND IT WILL BE GIVEN TO YOU; SEEK, AND YOU WILL FIND;
KNOCK, AND IT WILL BE OPENED TO YOU.

MATTHEW 7:7

Rejoice evermore.
Pray without ceasing.
In every thing give thanks,
for this is the will of God
in Christ Jesus
concerning you.

1 THESSALONIANS 5:16-18

Lord,
hear my prayers…

guide me to…

keep me grateful for…

help me hear your answers…

today's date

goals & notes for today

BE OF GOOD COURAGE, AND HE SHALL STRENGTHEN YOUR HEART,

ALL YE THAT HOPE IN THE LORD.

PSALM 31:24

Lord,

hear my prayers...

guide me to...

keep me grateful for...

help me hear your answers...

today's date

goals & notes for today

ASK, AND IT WILL BE GIVEN TO YOU; SEEK, AND YOU WILL FIND;

KNOCK, AND IT WILL BE OPENED TO YOU.

MATTHEW 7:7

Lord,

hear my prayers...

guide me to...

keep me grateful for...

help me hear your answers...

goals & notes for today

WATCH! STAND FIRM IN THE FAITH!

BE COURAGEOUS! BE STRONG!

1 CORINTHIANS 16:13

Lord,

hear my prayers...

guide me to...

keep me grateful for...

help me hear your answers...

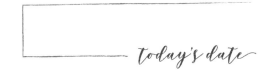

today's date

goals & notes for today

IN NOTHING BE ANXIOUS, BUT IN EVERYTHING,

BY PRAYER AND PETITION WITH THANKSGIVING,

LET YOUR REQUESTS BE MADE KNOWN TO GOD.

PHILIPPIANS 4:6

Lord,

hear my prayers...

guide me to...

keep me grateful for...

help me hear your answers...

today's date

goals & notes for today

THE LORD IS MY LIGHT AND MY SALVATION; WHOM SHALL I FEAR?
THE LORD IS THE STRENGTH OF MY LIFE; OF WHOM SHALL I BE AFRAID?

PSALM 27:1

Lord,

hear my prayers...

guide me to...

keep me grateful for...

help me hear your answers...

today's date

goals & notes for today

AND WHATSOEVER YE SHALL ASK IN MY NAME, THAT WILL I DO,

THAT THE FATHER MAY BE GLORIFIED IN THE SON.

JOHN 14:13

Lord,

hear my prayers... _____

_____

guide me to... _____

_____

keep me grateful for... _____

_____

help me hear your answers... _____

_____

today's date

goals & notes for today

BUT THANKS BE TO GOD, WHO GIVES US THE VICTORY

THROUGH OUR LORD JESUS CHRIST.

1 CORINTHIANS 15:57

Lord,

hear my prayers...

guide me to...

keep me grateful for...

help me hear your answers...

today's date

goals & notes for today

I CAN DO ALL THINGS THROUGH CHRIST, WHO STRENGTHENS ME.

PHILIPPIANS 4:13

Lord,

hear my prayers...

guide me to...

keep me grateful for...

help me hear your answers...

today's date

goals & notes for today

GOD IS OUR REFUGE AND STRENGTH,

A VERY PRESENT HELP IN TROUBLE.

PSALM 46:1

Lord,
hear my prayers...

guide me to...

keep me grateful for...

help me hear your answers...

today's date

goals & notes for today

I CRIED UNTO HIM WITH MY MOUTH,

AND HE WAS EXTOLLED WITH MY TONGUE.

PSALM 66:17

Lord,

hear my prayers... ⸻

guide me to... ⸻

keep me grateful for... ⸻

help me hear your answers... ⸻

today's date

goals & notes for today

YE ARE OF GOD, LITTLE CHILDREN, AND HAVE OVERCOME THEM:
BECAUSE GREATER IS HE THAT IS IN YOU, THAN HE THAT IS IN THE WORLD.

1 JOHN 4:4

Lord,

hear my prayers...

guide me to...

keep me grateful for...

help me hear your answers...

today's date

goals & notes for today

I HAVE SET THE LORD ALWAYS BEFORE ME:

BECAUSE HE IS AT MY RIGHT HAND, I SHALL NOT BE MOVED.

PSALM 16:8

Lord,

hear my prayers...

guide me to...

keep me grateful for...

help me hear your answers...

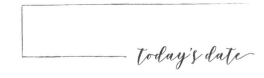

today's date

goals & notes for today

THIS HOPE WE HAVE AS AN ANCHOR OF THE SOUL,

A HOPE BOTH SURE AND STEADFAST

HEBREWS 6:19

Lord,

hear my prayers...

guide me to...

keep me grateful for...

help me hear your answers...

today's date

goals & notes for today

CONTINUE IN PRAYER, AND WATCH IN THE SAME WITH THANKSGIVING

COLOSSIANS 4:2

Lord,

hear my prayers...

guide me to...

keep me grateful for...

help me hear your answers...

today's date

goals & notes for today

IS ANY AMONG YOU SUFFERING? LET HIM PRAY.

IS ANY CHEERFUL? LET HIM SING PRAISES.

JAMES 5:13

Lord,
hear my prayers...

guide me to...

keep me grateful for...

help me hear your answers...

today's date

goals & notes for today

THIS IS MY COMFORT IN MY AFFLICTION,

FOR YOUR WORD HAS REVIVED ME.

PSALM 119:50

Lord,
hear my prayers…

guide me to…

keep me grateful for…

help me hear your answers…

today's date

goals & notes for today

FOR WITH GOD NOTHING SHALL BE IMPOSSIBLE.

LUKE 1:37

Lord,

hear my prayers...

_____

_____

guide me to...

_____

keep me grateful for...

_____

help me hear your answers...

_____

today's date

goals & notes for today

BUT LET HIM ASK IN FAITH, WITHOUT ANY DOUBTING,

FOR HE WHO DOUBTS IS LIKE A WAVE OF THE SEA,

DRIVEN BY THE WIND AND TOSSED.

JAMES 1:6

Lord,

hear my prayers…

guide me to…

keep me grateful for…

help me hear your answers…

today's date

goals & notes for today

IN MY DISTRESS I CALLED UPON THE LORD, AND CRIED UNTO MY GOD:

HE HEARD MY VOICE OUT OF HIS TEMPLE,

AND MY CRY CAME BEFORE HIM, EVEN INTO HIS EARS.

PSALM 18:6

Lord,

hear my prayers...

guide me to...

keep me grateful for...

help me hear your answers...

today's date

goals & notes for today

Come to me, all you who labor and are heavily burdened,

and I will give you rest.

Matthew 11:28

Lord,

hear my prayers...

guide me to...

keep me grateful for...

help me hear your answers...

goals & notes for today

BUT KNOW THAT THE LORD HATH SET APART HIM THAT IS GODLY
FOR HIMSELF: THE LORD WILL HEAR WHEN I CALL UNTO HIM.

PSALMS 4:3

Lord,

hear my prayers…

guide me to…

keep me grateful for…

help me hear your answers…

today's date

goals & notes for today

But I tell you, love your enemies, bless those who curse you,

do good to those who hate you,

and pray for those who mistreat you and persecute you

Matthew 5:44

Lord,

hear my prayers...

guide me to...

keep me grateful for...

help me hear your answers...

today's date

goals & notes for today

FOR I KNOW THE THOUGHTS THAT I THINK TOWARD YOU,
SAITH THE LORD, THOUGHTS OF PEACE, AND NOT OF EVIL,
TO GIVE YOU AN EXPECTED END.

JEREMIAH 29:11

Lord,

hear my prayers...

guide me to...

keep me grateful for...

help me hear your answers...

today's date

goals & notes for today

THEREFORE EXHORT ONE ANOTHER,

AND BUILD EACH OTHER UP, EVEN AS YOU ALSO DO.

1 THESSALONIANS 5:11

Lord,

hear my prayers... —————————

—————————————————————

guide me to... —————————

—————————————————————

keep me grateful for... —————————

—————————————————————

help me hear your answers... —————————

today's date

goals & notes for today

THE NAME OF THE LORD IS A STRONG TOWER:

THE RIGHTEOUS RUNNETH INTO IT, AND IS SAFE.

PROVERBS 18:10

Lord,

hear my prayers...

guide me to...

keep me grateful for...

help me hear your answers...

today's date

goals & notes for today

BEING CONFIDENT OF THIS VERY THING,

THAT HE WHICH HATH BEGUN A GOOD WORK IN YOU

WILL PERFORM IT UNTIL THE DAY OF JESUS CHRIST.

PHILIPPIANS 1:6

Lord,

hear my prayers...

guide me to...

keep me grateful for...

help me hear your answers...

today's date

goals & notes for today

AND HE SAID UNTO THEM,

THIS KIND CAN COME FORTH BY NOTHING, BUT BY PRAYER AND FASTING.

MARK 9:29

Lord,

hear my prayers...

guide me to...

keep me grateful for...

help me hear your answers...

today's date

goals & notes for today

FEAR NOT, LITTLE FLOCK; FOR IT IS YOUR
FATHER'S GOOD PLEASURE TO GIVE YOU THE KINGDOM.

LUKE 12:32

Lord,

hear my prayers... —————————————

————————————————————————————————————

guide me to... ——————————————————

————————————————————————————————————

keep me grateful for... ———————————

————————————————————————————————————

help me hear your answers... ————————

————————————————————————————————————

today's date

goals & notes for today

Now faith is the substance of things hoped for,

the evidence of things not seen.

Hebrews 11:1

Lord,

hear my prayers… _____

_____

_____

guide me to… _____

_____

_____

keep me grateful for… _____

_____

_____

help me hear your answers… _____

_____

_____

today's date

goals & notes for today

LET YOUR CONVERSATION BE WITHOUT COVETOUSNESS;

AND BE CONTENT WITH SUCH THINGS AS YE HAVE: FOR HE HATH SAID,

I WILL NEVER LEAVE THEE, NOR FORSAKE THEE.

HEBREWS 13:5

Lord,

hear my prayers...

guide me to...

keep me grateful for...

help me hear your answers...

today's date

goals & notes for today

ANSWER ME WHEN I CALL, GOD OF MY RIGHTEOUSNESS.

GIVE ME RELIEF FROM MY DISTRESS.

HAVE MERCY ON ME, AND HEAR MY PRAYER.

PSALM 4:1

Lord,
hear my prayers...

guide me to...

keep me grateful for...

help me hear your answers...

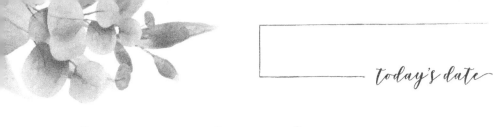

today's date

goals & notes for today

You shall call on me, and you shall go and pray to me,

and I will listen to you.

Lord,

hear my prayers...

guide me to...

keep me grateful for...

help me hear your answers...

today's date

goals & notes for today

THE GRACE OF OUR LORD JESUS CHRIST BE WITH YOU. AMEN.

1 THESSALONIANS 5:28

Lord,

hear my prayers...

guide me to...

keep me grateful for...

help me hear your answers...

today's date

goals & notes for today

SEEK THE LORD AND HIS STRENGTH, SEEK HIS FACE CONTINUALLY.

1 CHRONICLES 16:11

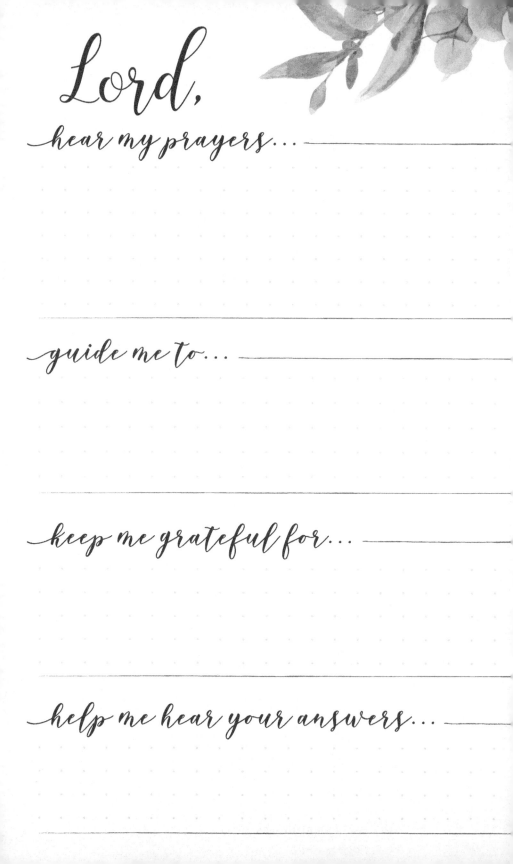

Lord,
hear my prayers... _____

_____

guide me to... _____

_____

keep me grateful for... _____

_____

help me hear your answers... _____

_____

today's date

goals & notes for today

IN MY DISTRESS I CRIED UNTO THE LORD, AND HE HEARD ME.

PSALM 120:1

Lord,

hear my prayers...

_____

guide me to...

_____

keep me grateful for...

_____

help me hear your answers...

_____

today's date

goals & notes for today

THE LORD IS NEAR TO ALL WHO CALL ON HIM,

TO ALL WHO CALL ON HIM IN TRUTH.

PSALM 145:18

Lord,

hear my prayers... ―――――――――

guide me to... ―――――――――

keep me grateful for... ―――――――

help me hear your answers... ―――――

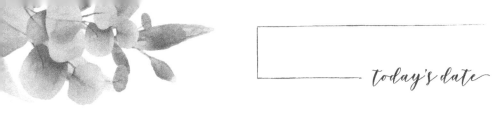

today's date

goals & notes for today

THE STEPS OF A GOOD MAN ARE ORDERED BY THE LORD:
AND HE DELIGHTETH IN HIS WAY. THOUGH HE FALL, HE SHALL NOT BE
UTTERLY CAST DOWN: FOR THE LORD UPHOLDETH HIM WITH HIS HAND.

PSALM 37:23-24

Lord,

hear my prayers...

guide me to...

keep me grateful for...

help me hear your answers...

today's date

goals & notes for today

CALL UNTO ME, AND I WILL ANSWER THEE,
AND SHOW THEE GREAT AND MIGHTY THINGS,
WHICH THOU KNOWEST NOT.

JEREMIAH 33:3

Lord,

hear my prayers...

guide me to...

keep me grateful for...

help me hear your answers...

today's date

goals & notes for today

YET THE LORD WILL COMMAND HIS LOVINGKINDNESS IN THE DAY TIME,

AND IN THE NIGHT HIS SONG SHALL BE WITH ME,

AND MY PRAYER UNTO THE GOD OF MY LIFE.

PSALM 42:8

Lord,

hear my prayers...

guide me to...

keep me grateful for...

help me hear your answers...

today's date

goals & notes for today

AND WE KNOW THAT ALL THINGS WORK TOGETHER FOR GOOD
TO THEM THAT LOVE GOD, TO THEM WHO ARE THE CALLED
ACCORDING TO HIS PURPOSE.

ROMANS 8:28

Lord,

hear my prayers... ————————————

guide me to... ————————————

keep me grateful for... ————————————

help me hear your answers... ————————————

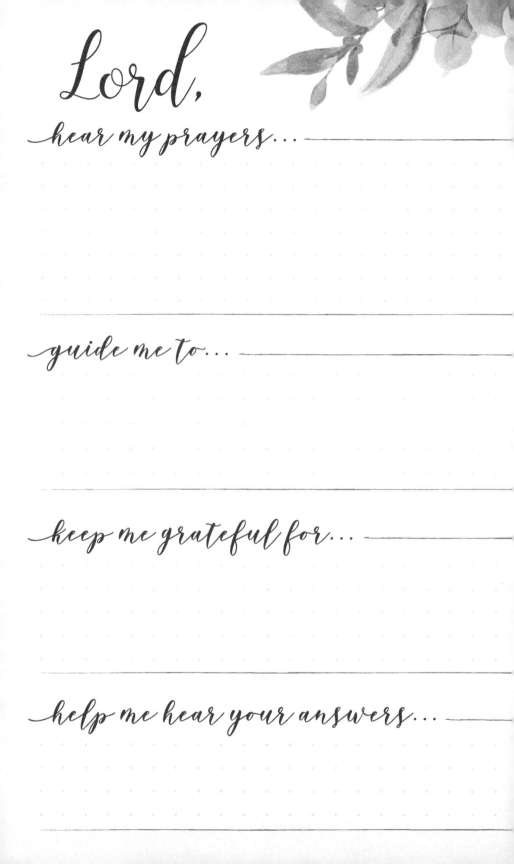

today's date

goals & notes for today

THE LIGHT SHINES IN THE DARKNESS,
AND THE DARKNESS HASN'T OVERCOME IT.

JOHN 1:5

Lord,

hear my prayers...

guide me to...

keep me grateful for...

help me hear your answers...

today's date

goals & notes for today

CALL ON ME IN THE DAY OF TROUBLE.

I WILL DELIVER YOU, AND YOU WILL HONOR ME.

PSALM 50:15

Lord,

hear my prayers… _____

_____

guide me to… _____

_____

keep me grateful for… _____

_____

help me hear your answers… _____

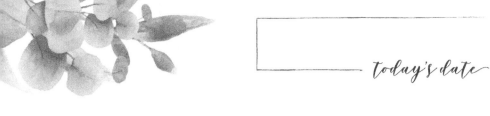

today's date

goals & notes for today

NOW MAY THE GOD OF HOPE FILL YOU WITH ALL JOY
AND PEACE IN BELIEVING, THAT YOU MAY ABOUND IN HOPE,
IN THE POWER OF THE HOLY SPIRIT.

ROMANS 15:13

Lord,

hear my prayers...

guide me to...

keep me grateful for...

help me hear your answers...

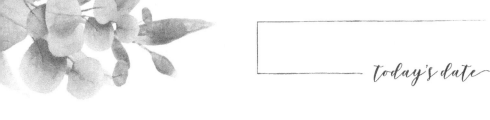

goals & notes for today

CONFESS YOUR OFFENSES TO ONE ANOTHER,

AND PRAY FOR ONE ANOTHER, THAT YOU MAY BE HEALED.

THE INSISTENT PRAYER OF A RIGHTEOUS PERSON IS POWERFULLY EFFECTIVE.

JAMES 5:16

Lord,

hear my prayers...

guide me to...

keep me grateful for...

help me hear your answers...

goals & notes for today

NOW MAY THE LORD OF PEACE HIMSELF

GIVE YOU PEACE AT ALL TIMES IN ALL WAYS.

THE LORD BE WITH YOU ALL.

2 THESSALONIANS 3:16

Lord,

hear my prayers...

guide me to...

keep me grateful for...

help me hear your answers...

today's date

goals & notes for today

IF YOU REMAIN IN ME, AND MY WORDS REMAIN IN YOU,

YOU WILL ASK WHATEVER YOU DESIRE, AND IT WILL BE DONE FOR YOU.

JOHN 15:7

Lord,
hear my prayers... ———————

guide me to... ———————

keep me grateful for... ———————

help me hear your answers... ———

today's date

goals & notes for today

THE LORD IS MY STRENGTH AND MY DEFENCE;

HE HAS BECOME MY SALVATION.

PSALM 118:14

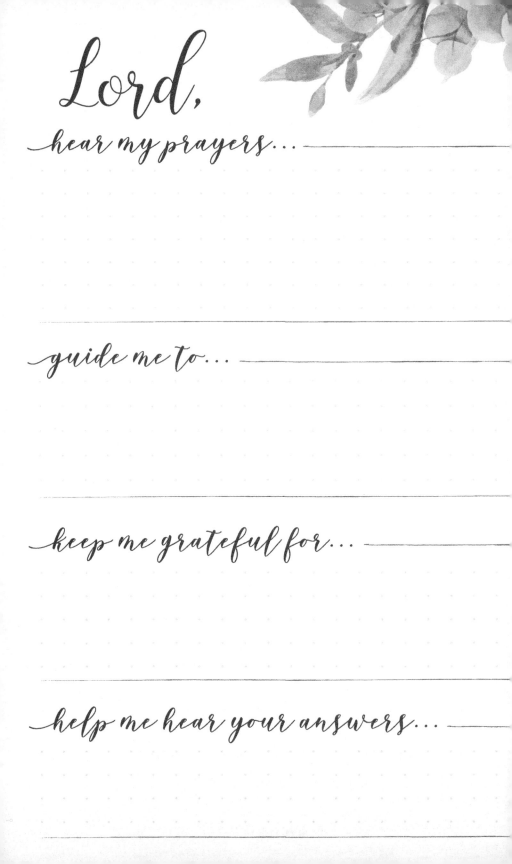

Lord,

hear my prayers...

guide me to...

keep me grateful for...

help me hear your answers...

today's date

goals & notes for today

JESUS LOOKED AT THEM AND SAID,

"WITH MAN THIS IS IMPOSSIBLE, BUT NOT WITH GOD;

ALL THINGS ARE POSSIBLE WITH GOD."

MARK 10:27

Lord,

hear my prayers...

guide me to...

keep me grateful for...

help me hear your answers...

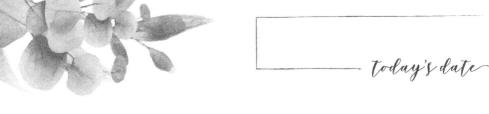

today's date

goals & notes for today

HE WILL WIPE AWAY FROM THEM EVERY TEAR FROM THEIR EYES. DEATH
WILL BE NO MORE; NEITHER WILL THERE BE MOURNING, NOR CRYING,
NOR PAIN, ANY MORE. THE FIRST THINGS HAVE PASSED AWAY.

REVELATION 21:4

Lord,

hear my prayers...

guide me to...

keep me grateful for...

help me hear your answers...

today's date

goals & notes for today

MY VOICE SHALT THOU HEAR IN THE MORNING, O LORD; IN THE
MORNING WILL I DIRECT MY PRAYER UNTO THEE, AND WILL LOOK UP.

PSALM 5:3

Lord,

hear my prayers...

guide me to...

keep me grateful for...

help me hear your answers...

today's date

goals & notes for today

THIS IS THE BOLDNESS WHICH WE HAVE TOWARD HIM,

THAT, IF WE ASK ANYTHING ACCORDING TO HIS WILL, HE LISTENS TO US.

1 JOHN 5:14

Lord,

hear my prayers...

guide me to...

keep me grateful for...

help me hear your answers...

today's date

goals & notes for today

LET US NOT BE WEARY IN DOING GOOD,

FOR WE WILL REAP IN DUE SEASON, IF WE DON'T GIVE UP.

GALATIANS 6:9

Lord,

hear my prayers... ―――――――

―――――――

guide me to... ―――――――

―――――――

keep me grateful for... ―――――――

―――――――

help me hear your answers... ―――――――

―――――――

today's date

goals & notes for today

I THANK MY GOD ALWAYS ON YOUR BEHALF,

FOR THE GRACE OF GOD WHICH IS GIVEN YOU BY JESUS CHRIST.

1 CORINTHIANS 1:4

Lord,

hear my prayers...

guide me to...

keep me grateful for...

help me hear your answers...

today's date

goals & notes for today

CASTING ALL YOUR WORRIES ON HIM, BECAUSE HE CARES FOR YOU.

1 PETER 5:7

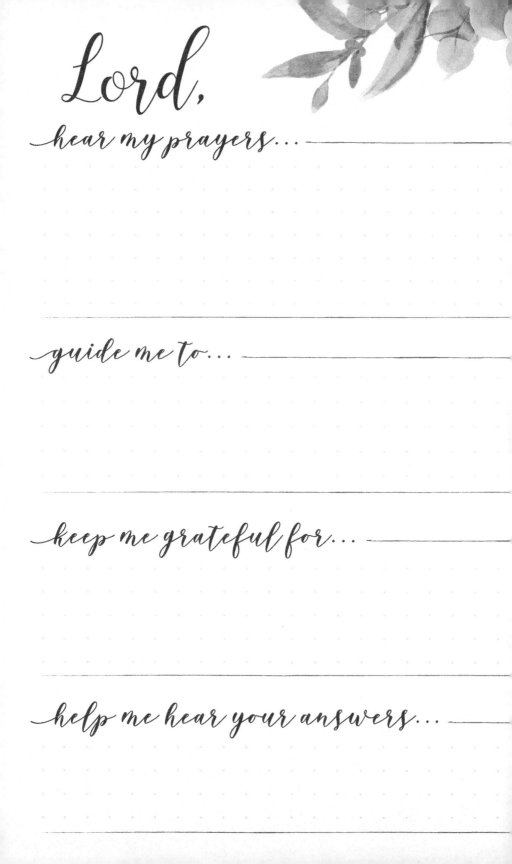

Lord,

hear my prayers... ———————————

guide me to... ———————————

keep me grateful for... ———————————

help me hear your answers... ———————

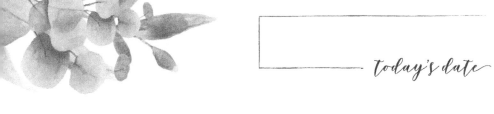

today's date

goals & notes for today

HE ALSO SPOKE A PARABLE TO THEM THAT THEY

MUST ALWAYS PRAY, AND NOT GIVE UP

LUKE 18:1

Lord,

hear my prayers...

guide me to...

keep me grateful for...

help me hear your answers...

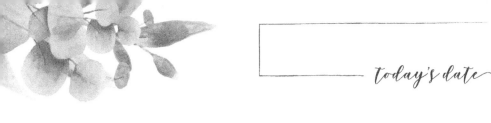

today's date

goals & notes for today

EVEN THOUGH I WALK THROUGH THE VALLEY OF THE SHADOW OF DEATH,

I WILL FEAR NO EVIL, FOR YOU ARE WITH ME;

YOUR ROD AND YOUR STAFF, THEY COMFORT ME.

PSALM 23:4

Lord,

hear my prayers...

guide me to...

keep me grateful for...

help me hear your answers...

today's date

goals & notes for today

LET MY PRAYER BE SET BEFORE YOU LIKE INCENSE;
THE LIFTING UP OF MY HANDS LIKE THE EVENING SACRIFICE.

PSALM 141:2

Lord,

hear my prayers...

guide me to...

keep me grateful for...

help me hear your answers...

today's date

goals & notes for today

WHAT THEN SHALL WE SAY ABOUT THESE THINGS?

IF GOD IS FOR US, WHO CAN BE AGAINST US?

ROMANS 8:31

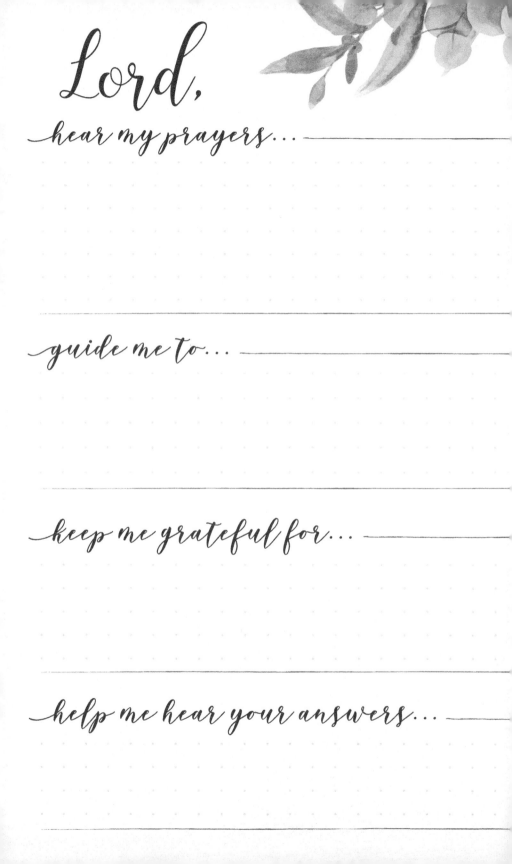

Lord,

hear my prayers... _____

_____

guide me to... _____

_____

keep me grateful for... _____

_____

help me hear your answers... _____

_____

today's date

goals & notes for today

LET US HOLD FAST THE CONFESSION OF OUR HOPE WITHOUT WAVERING;

FOR HE WHO PROMISED IS FAITHFUL.

HEBREWS 10:23

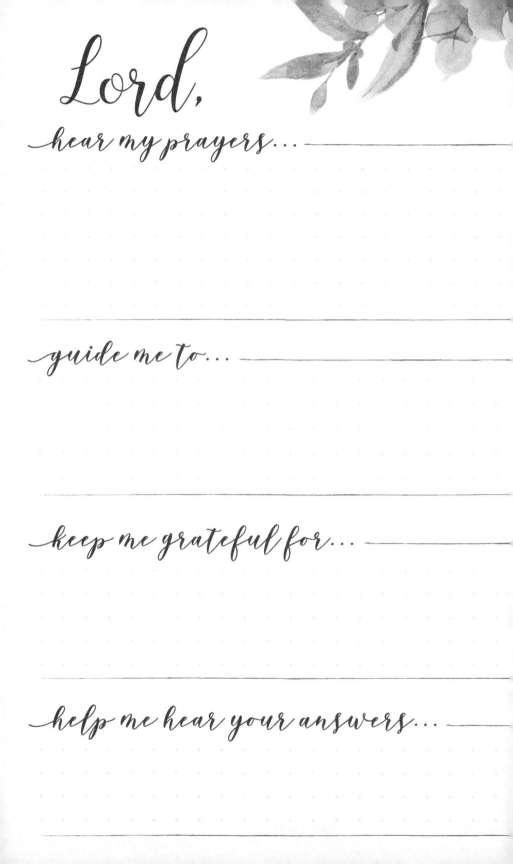

Lord,

hear my prayers...

guide me to...

keep me grateful for...

help me hear your answers...

goals & notes for today

S EEK YE THE L ORD WHILE HE MAY BE FOUND,

CALL YE UPON HIM WHILE HE IS NEAR

ISAIAH 55:6

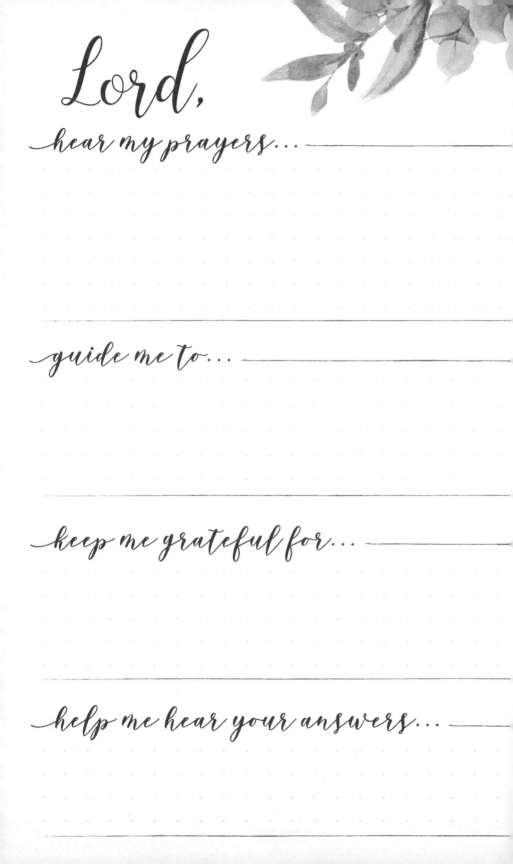

Lord,

hear my prayers... ————————

————————————————————

guide me to... ————————————

————————————————————

keep me grateful for... ——————

————————————————————

help me hear your answers... ———

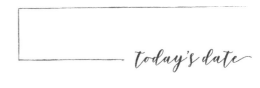

today's date

goals & notes for today

A<small>LL THINGS, WHATEVER YOU ASK IN PRAYER,</small>

B<small>ELIEVING, YOU WILL RECEIVE.</small>

M<small>ATTHEW 21:22</small>

Lord,

hear my prayers...

guide me to...

keep me grateful for...

help me hear your answers...

today's date

goals & notes for today

LET US THEREFORE COME BOLDLY UNTO THE THRONE OF GRACE,

THAT WE MAY OBTAIN MERCY, AND FIND GRACE TO HELP IN TIME OF NEED.

HEBREWS 4:16

Lord,

hear my prayers . . .

guide me to . . .

keep me grateful for . . .

help me hear your answers . . .

goals & notes for today

SET YOUR AFFECTION ON THINGS ABOVE,

NOT ON THINGS ON THE EARTH.

COLOSSIANS 3:2

Lord,

hear my prayers...

guide me to...

keep me grateful for...

help me hear your answers...

goals & notes for today

REJOICE EVERMORE. PRAY WITHOUT CEASING.

IN EVERY THING GIVE THANKS: FOR THIS IS THE WILL OF GOD

IN CHRIST JESUS CONCERNING YOU.

1 THESSALONIANS 5:16-18

Lord,

hear my prayers...

guide me to...

keep me grateful for...

help me hear your answers...

today's date

goals & notes for today

YOU WILL KEEP WHOEVER'S MIND IS STEADFAST IN PERFECT PEACE,

BECAUSE HE TRUSTS IN YOU.

ISAIAH 26:3

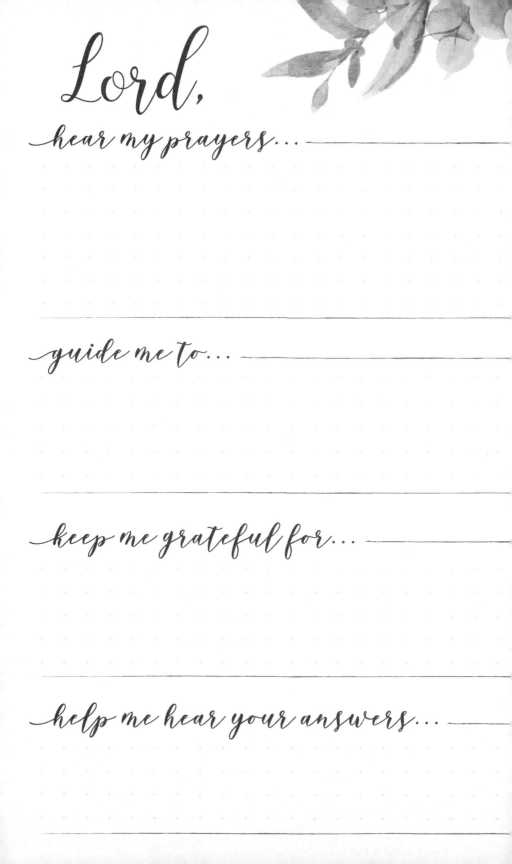

Lord,

hear my prayers…

guide me to…

keep me grateful for…

help me hear your answers…

today's date

goals & notes for today

He alone is my rock and my salvation, my fortress.

I will not be shaken.

Lord,

hear my prayers... ————————————

guide me to... ————————————

keep me grateful for... ————————————

help me hear your answers... ————

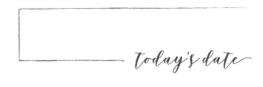

today's date

goals & notes for today

IF YOU FALTER IN THE TIME OF TROUBLE,

YOUR STRENGTH IS SMALL.

PROVERBS 24:10

Lord,

hear my prayers...

guide me to...

keep me grateful for...

help me hear your answers...

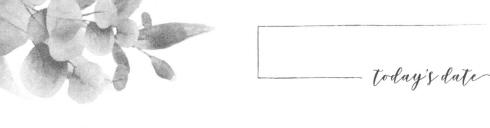

goals & notes for today

Whenever you stand praying, forgive,

if you have anything against anyone; so that your Father,

who is in heaven, may also forgive you your transgressions.

Mark 11:25

Lord,

hear my prayers...

guide me to...

keep me grateful for...

help me hear your answers...

today's date

goals & notes for today

WATCH AND PRAY, THAT YOU DON'T ENTER INTO TEMPTATION.

THE SPIRIT INDEED IS WILLING, BUT THE FLESH IS WEAK.

MATTHEW 26:41

Lord,

hear my prayers...

guide me to...

keep me grateful for...

help me hear your answers...

goals & notes for today

DON'T YOU BE AFRAID, FOR I AM WITH YOU.
DON'T BE DISMAYED, FOR I AM YOUR GOD. I WILL STRENGTHEN YOU.
YES, I WILL HELP YOU. YES, I WILL UPHOLD YOU WITH THE RIGHT HAND OF
MY RIGHTEOUSNESS.

ISAIAH 41:10

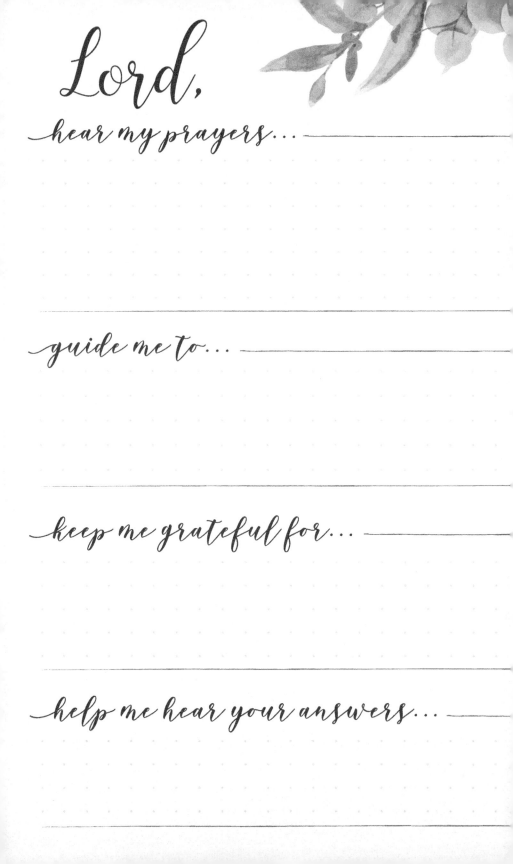

Lord,

hear my prayers...

guide me to...

keep me grateful for...

help me hear your answers...

goals & notes for today

My God will supply every need of yours

according to his riches in glory in Christ Jesus.

Philippians 4:19

Lord,
hear my prayers...

guide me to...

keep me grateful for...

help me hear your answers...

today's date

goals & notes for today

BUT YOU, WHEN YOU PRAY, ENTER INTO YOUR INNER ROOM,
AND HAVING SHUT YOUR DOOR, PRAY TO YOUR FATHER WHO IS IN SECRET,
AND YOUR FATHER WHO SEES IN SECRET WILL REWARD YOU OPENLY.

MATTHEW 6:6

Lord,

hear my prayers...

guide me to...

keep me grateful for...

help me hear your answers...

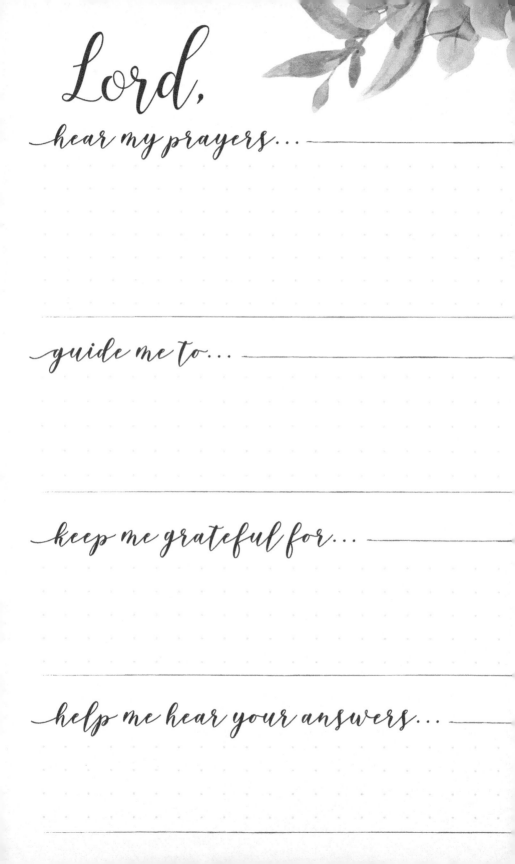

today's date

goals & notes for today

TRUST IN THE LORD WITH ALL THINE HEART;

AND LEAN NOT UNTO THINE OWN UNDERSTANDING.

IN ALL THY WAYS ACKNOWLEDGE HIM, AND HE SHALL DIRECT THY PATHS.

PROVERBS 3:5-6

Lord,

hear my prayers...

guide me to...

keep me grateful for...

help me hear your answers...

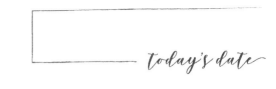

today's date

goals & notes for today

MANY ARE THE AFFLICTIONS OF THE RIGHTEOUS:

BUT THE LORD DELIVERETH HIM OUT OF THEM ALL.

PSALM 34:19

Lord,

hear my prayers...

guide me to...

keep me grateful for...

help me hear your answers...

today's date

goals & notes for today

HEAR MY PRAYER, O LORD, GIVE EAR TO MY SUPPLICATIONS:
IN THY FAITHFULNESS ANSWER ME, AND IN THY RIGHTEOUSNESS.

PSALM 143:1

Lord,

hear my prayers…

guide me to…

keep me grateful for…

help me hear your answers…

today's date

goals & notes for today

LET THE WORDS OF MY MOUTH, AND THE MEDITATION OF MY HEART,

BE ACCEPTABLE IN THY SIGHT, O LORD, MY STRENGTH, AND MY REDEEMER

PSALM 19:14

Lord,

hear my prayers... ─────────────

─────────────────────────

guide me to... ─────────────

─────────────────────────

keep me grateful for... ─────────

─────────────────────────

help me hear your answers... ──────

─────────────────────────

today's date

goals & notes for today

AND I SAY UNTO YOU, ASK, AND IT SHALL BE GIVEN YOU;

SEEK, AND YE SHALL FIND; KNOCK, AND IT SHALL BE OPENED UNTO YOU.

LUKE 11:9

Lord,

hear my prayers... _____

_____

guide me to... _____

_____

keep me grateful for... _____

_____

help me hear your answers... _____

today's date

goals & notes for today

REJOICING IN HOPE;

ENDURING IN TROUBLES;

CONTINUING STEADFASTLY IN PRAYER

ROMANS 12:12

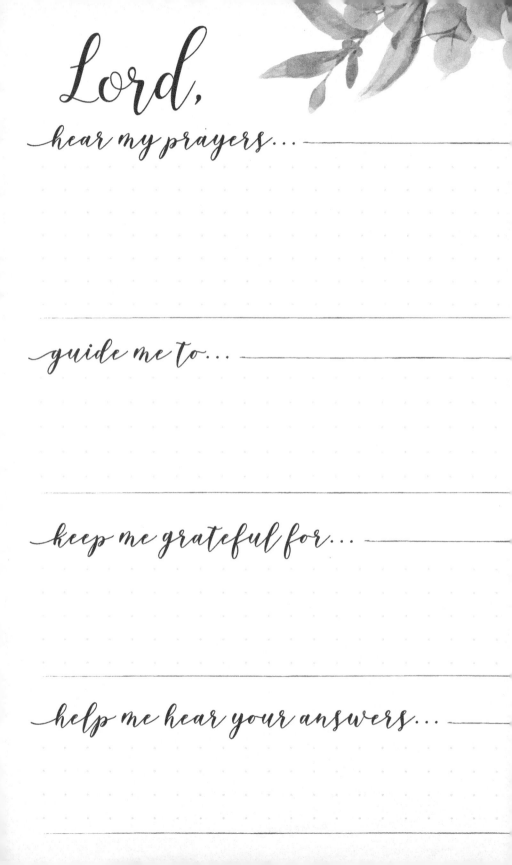

Lord,

hear my prayers… ————————

guide me to… ————————

keep me grateful for… ————————

help me hear your answers… ————————

today's date

goals & notes for today

AND THE PEACE OF GOD, WHICH SURPASSES ALL UNDERSTANDING,

WILL GUARD YOUR HEARTS AND YOUR THOUGHTS IN CHRIST JESUS.

PHILIPPIANS 4:7

Lord,

hear my prayers…

guide me to…

keep me grateful for…

help me hear your answers…

today's date

goals & notes for today

SAVE NOW, I BESEECH THEE, O LORD:

O LORD, I BESEECH THEE, SEND NOW PROSPERITY.

PSALM 118:25

Lord,

hear my prayers…

guide me to…

keep me grateful for…

help me hear your answers…

goals & notes for today

NOW MAY THE GOD OF HOPE FILL YOU WITH ALL JOY AND PEACE

IN BELIEVING, THAT YOU MAY ABOUND IN HOPE,

IN THE POWER OF THE HOLY SPIRIT.

ROMANS 15:13

Lord,

hear my prayers...

guide me to...

keep me grateful for...

help me hear your answers...

today's date

goals & notes for today

BUT THEY THAT WAIT UPON THE LORD SHALL RENEW THEIR STRENGTH;
THEY SHALL MOUNT UP WITH WINGS AS EAGLES; THEY SHALL RUN,
AND NOT BE WEARY; AND THEY SHALL WALK, AND NOT FAINT.

ISAIAH 40:31

Lord,

hear my prayers... _____

_____

_____

_____

_____

guide me to... _____

_____

_____

keep me grateful for... _____

_____

_____

help me hear your answers... _____

_____

_____

today's date

goals & notes for today

AND IF WE KNOW THAT HE LISTENS TO US, WHATEVER WE ASK,

WE KNOW THAT WE HAVE THE PETITIONS WHICH WE HAVE ASKED OF HIM.

1 JOHN 5:15

Lord,

hear my prayers… —————————

guide me to… —————————

keep me grateful for… —————————

help me hear your answers… —————————

today's date

goals & notes for today

BE NOT OVERCOME OF EVIL, BUT OVERCOME EVIL WITH GOOD.

ROMANS 12:21

Lord,

hear my prayers… ────────────

───────────────────────

guide me to… ────────────────

───────────────────────

keep me grateful for… ──────────

───────────────────────

help me hear your answers… ──────

today's date

goals & notes for today

THEREFORE I TELL YOU, ALL THINGS WHATEVER YOU PRAY AND ASK FOR,

BELIEVE THAT YOU HAVE RECEIVED THEM, AND YOU SHALL HAVE THEM.

MARK 11:24

Lord,

hear my prayers...

guide me to...

keep me grateful for...

help me hear your answers...

goals & notes for today

PEACE I LEAVE WITH YOU. MY PEACE I GIVE TO YOU;

NOT AS THE WORLD GIVES, GIVE I TO YOU.

DON'T LET YOUR HEART BE TROUBLED, NEITHER LET IT BE FEARFUL.

JOHN 14:27

Lord,
hear my prayers...

guide me to...

keep me grateful for...

help me hear your answers...

today's date

goals & notes for today

CAST THY BURDEN UPON THE LORD, AND HE SHALL SUSTAIN THEE:

HE SHALL NEVER SUFFER THE RIGHTEOUS TO BE MOVED.

PSALM 55:22

Lord,

hear my prayers…

guide me to…

keep me grateful for…

help me hear your answers…

today's date

goals & notes for today

HAVE NOT I COMMANDED THEE? BE STRONG AND OF A GOOD COURAGE;

BE NOT AFRAID, NEITHER BE THOU DISMAYED:

FOR THE LORD THY GOD IS WITH THEE WHITHERSOEVER THOU GOEST.

JOSHUA 1:9

Lord,

hear my prayers...

guide me to...

keep me grateful for...

help me hear your answers...

today's date

goals & notes for today

T<small>AKE MY YOKE UPON YOU, AND LEARN FROM ME, FOR</small> I <small>AM GENTLE
AND HUMBLE IN HEART; AND YOU WILL FIND REST FOR YOUR SOULS.
FOR MY YOKE IS EASY, AND MY BURDEN IS LIGHT.</small>

M<small>ATTHEW</small> 11:29-30

Lord,

hear my prayers...

guide me to...

keep me grateful for...

help me hear your answers...

today's date

goals & notes for today

THEREFORE DON'T BE ANXIOUS FOR TOMORROW,

FOR TOMORROW WILL BE ANXIOUS FOR ITSELF.

MATTHEW 6:34A

Made in the USA
Middletown, DE
02 October 2023

39944998R00104